A Small Affair

A comedy

Bob Larbey

Samuel French — London
New York - Toronto - Hollywood

© 1994 BY BOB LARBEY

Rights of Performance by Amateurs are controlled by Samuel French Ltd, 52 Fitzroy Street, London W1P 6JR, and they, or their authorized agents, issue licences to amateurs on payment of a fee. **It is an infringement of the Copyright to give any performance or public reading of the play before the fee has been paid and the licence issued.**

The Royalty Fee indicated below is subject to contract and subject to variation at the sole discretion of Samuel French Ltd.

Basic fee for each and every
performance by amateurs   Code G
in the British Isles

The Professional Rights in this play are controlled by Lemon Unna and Durbridge Ltd, 24 Pottery Lane, Holland Park, London W11 4LZ

The publication of this play does not imply that it is necessarily available for performance by amateurs or professionals, either in the British Isles or Overseas. Amateurs and professionals considering a production are strongly advised in their own interests to apply to the appropriate agents for consent before starting rehearsals or booking a theatre or hall.

ISBN 0 573 12135 4

Please see page iv for further copyright information

CHARACTERS

Guy
Judy
Terry
Ellen
Harry
Mona
Janet
Ada
Harriet
Caroline
Mrs Hodge
Mrs Webb
Mrs Platt
Ron
Stevie
Sally
Head of Drama

The action of the play takes place in a TV rehearsal room

Time: the present

COPYRIGHT INFORMATION

(See also page ii)

This play is fully protected under the Copyright Laws of the British Commonwealth of Nations, the United States of America and all countries of the Berne and Universal Copyright Conventions.

All rights including Stage, Motion Picture, Radio, Television, Public Reading, and Translation into Foreign Languages, are strictly reserved.

No part of this publication may lawfully be reproduced in ANY form or by any means — photocopying, typescript, recording (including video-recording), manuscript, electronic, mechanical, or otherwise—or be transmitted or stored in a retrieval system, without prior permission.

Licences for amateur performances are issued subject to the understanding that it shall be made clear in all advertising matter that the audience will witness an amateur performance; that the names of the authors of the plays shall be included on all programmes; and that the integrity of the authors' work will be preserved.

The Royalty Fee is subject to contract and subject to variation at the sole discretion of Samuel French Ltd.

In Theatres or Halls seating Four Hundred or more the fee will be subject to negotiation.

In Territories Overseas the fee quoted above may not apply. A fee will be quoted on application to our local authorized agent, or if there is no such agent, on application to Samuel French Ltd, London.

VIDEO-RECORDING OF AMATEUR PRODUCTIONS

Please note that the copyright laws governing video-recording are extremely complex and that it should not be assumed that any play may be video-recorded for whatever purpose without first obtaining the permission of the appropriate agents. The fact that a play is published by Samuel French Ltd does not indicate that video rights are available or that Samuel French Ltd controls such rights.

Other plays by Bob Larbey published by
Samuel French Ltd:

Building Blocks

Half an Idea

A Small Affair may be presented as a double bill with *Half An Idea*, using many of the same cast, to create a full evening's entertainment. Performance fees for the double bill will be given on application to Samuel French Ltd.

A SMALL AFFAIR

As the CURTAINS *opens, we see a television rehearsal room. It is not a glorious place at all, but fairly dingy. Some chairs are set against a wall, a small table is set nearby. On it is an electric kettle, a jar of coffee, a bag of sugar, a tin of biscuits, plastic spoons and lots of paper cups. Another small, wheeled table is nearby. On it is the floor manager's script, a stopwatch, and a little tub of different coloured pens. An internal telephone is on the wall. The working part of the room is divided into two sets. One is a Prison Governor's Office; the other, a Condemned Cell. Furnishings are sparse, in some cases, makeshift*

Judy, a floor manager, is putting the finishing touches to marking out the floor plan of the sets with coloured tape. She looks like a floor manager used to calming hysterical directors

Guy, a potentially hysterical director, enters. He wears a cravat, a cardigan over his shoulders and a faintly Sixties shirt to prove that he works in television. He carries an executive briefcase. He looks at the rehearsal room and drops the case dramatically

Guy Well, this is absurd! It's ridiculous! It's minuscule!
Judy Good-morning, Guy. Coffee?
Guy How can I drink coffee when they've given me a rabbit-hutch to rehearse in? Two sugars please, Judy.

Judy makes him a cup of coffee. Guy poses discontentedly around

Well, I'm not having it. I'm not standing for it. Get on to Drama and say I'm not standing for it.
Judy I already have—and you are.
Guy Oh? Who says so?
Judy The Head of Drama.
Guy I could make an issue of this.
Judy He advised that you shouldn't make an issue out of this.

Guy Those were his words?
Judy Paraphrased. He's up to his eyeballs, Guy. He's got six plays rehearsing at the same time and he's totally strapped for space. He also pointed out that ours isn't a *big* play.
Guy It would take a man with a small mind to say that. I've half a mind to phone him.

Judy points to the phone. Guy hesitates

> More than half a mind! (*He approaches the telephone as though it might bite him. He is about to pick it up when:*)

The phone rings

> (*He jumps, then recovers and answers it*) Guy Green. She's what? Why didn't you tell me? So you have. I'll be down. (*He hangs up*) Mona's here!

Judy Shall I order a brass band?

Guy heads towards the door

Guy Judy, she's a star. She's worked in Hollywood.
Judy So did Lassie!

Guy hurries out

Guy (*off*) Terry! You look wonderful!

Terry sighs a long moan off stage

> *Terry enters, moaning. He is an ageing actor. He has the mother and father of all hangovers and wears dark glasses. He carries a small bag*

Judy Terry, how nice to see you again.
Terry Where are you?

Judy goes up to him

Judy Just here.

A Small Affair

Terry Hallo, Judy.
Judy How are you?
Terry Worse than I look.
Judy That bad?
Terry Learn the words. I really did mean to learn the words last night.
Judy Then you had a drink or two?
Terry Or seven.
Judy Have a coffee.
Terry I'd prefer euthanasia.

Judy puts a chair under him and he slumps into it. She makes him a coffee

Ellen comes in. She is an emotional middle-aged actress

Ellen I've been in the loo...
Judy Oh, good. Coffee?

Ellen nods

How's Bill?

Ellen shakes her head to indicate that she cannot talk about him. Judy thinks it's going to be one of those days

Terry Hallo, Ellen. I'd get up, but I don't think I can.

Ellen gets herself a chair and sits

Judy Coffee up! (*She takes a cup to Ellen*)
Ellen He trod on my bifocals last night.
Judy Deliberately?
Ellen I don't know! That's the thing, I don't know!
Judy Would you like a biscuit?
Ellen Should I? I don't know.
Judy They're on the table, if you want one. (*She takes Terry his coffee*) Terry?

He takes the paper cup

Terry I sound like a boy, don't I?

Judy No, you've got a nice manly voice.
Terry Being called Terry, I mean. Terry Banks. It sounds like some spotty yob in *EastEnders*. I should be called Terence. Terence Banks!

Ellen decides to have a biscuit and crosses to get one

Ellen No-one would know who you are.
Terry No-one remembers who I was. (*He fumbles in his bag and takes out half a bottle of brandy*)
Judy Is that wise?
Terry Essential. (*He pours brandy into his coffee*)

Ellen takes the lid off the biscuit tin

Ellen Shall I have a Custard Cream or a Garibaldi?
Judy Mona's here, by the way.

Ellen puts the lid back on the biscuit tin. Terry takes a long swig of his laced coffee

Terry That's better. I still can't see the other side of the room, though.

Judy takes off his dark glasses

Ah, there it is. What are we rehearsing in—a Wendy house?

Janet comes in. She is about Ellen's age, but smarter, a very together lady

Ellen Mona won't like it.
Janet Mona's being buttered up. Mona is having lemon tea in the Green Room. Mona has been to Hollywood—in case anyone didn't know.
Ellen She did make a film.
Janet Yes. A film. One film in four years.
Judy Did anyone ever see it?
Terry I don't think it was released over here.
Janet She's probably very big in Albania.

Guy enters. He is very nervous

Guy Mona's here! Mona's here, everyone!

Janet All kneel!

Mona enters. She thinks she is twenty-eight, but she is not. She thinks she is a great star, which she is not. She opens her arms wide, almost hitting Guy in the face

Mona Good-morning, my sweets, good-morning!
All Good-morning, Mona.
Guy A chair for Mona, please, Judy.

Judy looks daggers, but picks up a chair

Mona No, no, no. I want to be treated like everyone else.
Judy Good. (*She puts the chair down*)

This is not quite what Mona had expected, but she gets herself a chair and sits

Ellen Would you like a biscuit, Mona?
Mona I daren't. I'm still on a California Diet.
Janet That's a long way to go for your meals.

Mona smiles. She obviously cannot stand Janet. Janet smiles back. The feeling is mutual

Guy (*quickly*) Well, here we are, boys and girls. Now, it's my belief that this play——
Mona Are we reading it through again?
Guy No, Mona, we did that yesterday. As I was saying, it's my belief that this play——
Mona Then why aren't we in the rehearsal room, Guy?

This produces a hush as the others wait for Guy to answer

Guy Well, the thing is, Mona, we are.
Mona You mean, this is it?
Guy Broadly speaking, yes.

Mona gets up

Mona I shall be in the Green Room!

She exits

Guy Mona! (*He looks round helplessly. Appealingly*) Judy?
Judy No, thanks.

Guy sighs and goes out after Mona

Terry Shall we go home or what?
Ellen I suppose if you're a star...
Janet As opposed to an actress.
Ellen Now, that's not fair, Janet. She was wonderful in *Howard's Way*.
Janet The boat acted better than her in *Howard's Way*.
Judy Jealous?
Janet Of course.

Terry gets up

Terry I think I'll have a tinkle.

He goes out

Ellen He looks awful, doesn't he?
Judy You should have seen him when he came in.
Janet Oh, he's a trouper, old Terry. A good actor too—once.
Ellen How is he with lines these days?
Judy A bit like trains. Occasionally they're on time, sometimes they're late—sometimes they never come at all.
Janet Well, he doesn't have much to do. It's a three-hander really.
Judy Not the way Mona sees it.
Ellen Be realistic, Judy. She is a name. I've never been a name. I've always been "I know the face".
Judy There are worse things to be.
Janet Like out of work. Do you know, I haven't done a telly since an episode of *The Bill* six months ago.
Ellen I must have missed that.
Janet That's what everybody says.

Mona and Guy enter, the best of friends

A Small Affair

Mona I didn't walk out for me. I walked out for all of us.
Janet And now you've walked back in for all of us.
Guy Mona's been an angel. I explained the situation and she's risen above it.
Janet On wings, presumably?
Mona (*sweetly*) May I have a word, Guy?
Guy Yes, of course.

They go out

Terry comes in

Terry Are we breaking for lunch?
Judy We haven't started yet.
Ellen (*offering the tin*) Have a biscuit.
Terry What I'd really like is a sherbet dab.
Judy Well, isn't that strange? I don't have any sherbet dabs.
Terry I could pop out.
Ellen Terry, just say "No."
Terry To what?
Ellen We all know the pubs are open.

Terry sits disconsolately

(*To Janet*) I shouldn't have said that, should I?

Janet is looking at the door

Janet?

Guy and Mona enter, Mona looking triumphant

Guy Could you spare me a second please, Janet? Take five, everyone!
Judy We haven't started yet.
Guy All right, Judy!

Guy takes Janet to a corner of the room

It's got to stop, Janet. Mona can't work under these conditions.

Janet Me being the conditions, presumably?
Guy She is the star.

Janet sighs heavily

And I hate to say this, Janet, but you *can* be replaced.
Janet Sorry, sorry, sorry.
Guy Good girl. Now, give me a big cuddle.

Janet allows herself to be cuddled

Right, everybody! Now, let's get to work, work, work!

Everyone stands up in anticipation

Harry, a workman, enters. He wears overalls and carries a bag of tools. He whistles loudly and tunelessly, nodding and winking cheerfully as a greeting. He sets his toolbag down with a thump. He spots the coffee things and sets about making himself a cup

The others all stare

Judy?

Judy goes up to Harry

Judy Good-morning.
Harry Hallo, luv.
Judy We are rehearsing.
Harry That's all right. Don't mind me. You carry on.

Guy stalks over

Guy Look, who are you?
Harry Harry.
Guy I mean, *what* are you?
Harry Maintenance.
Guy Well, what do you maintain?
Harry Everything in this building. You name it, I maintain it.

Guy turns away

Guy Ask him why he's here, Judy.
Judy Why are you here?
Harry Electrics. (*He points*) Here, I know you.
Mona (*preening*) I thought you might.
Harry No, not you. (*To Janet*) You. I saw you in *The Bill*.
Janet (*pleased*) Did you?
Harry Yes. In *The Bill*. Very good, you was, too. Very believable.
Janet Thank you.
Guy *What* electrics?

Harry points L to the toilets

Harry In there. Something's shorting on my visual display and that's where it is.
Terry I did hear a buzzing, but I thought it was just me.
Harry Dead give-away, a buzzing.
Guy Look, do you have to do it now?
Harry Well, unless you want the next person who pulls the chain to go up in a sheet of flames, yes.
Judy But you will be in there?
Harry Oh yes. As soon as I've drunk my coffee.
Ellen Would you like a biscuit?
Harry That's very kind of you, love.
Guy Ellen!
Ellen What?
Guy I would like to start.
Ellen Well, I'm ready.
Guy Fine. Good. Judy, be a love and show us the sets, would you?

Judy moves to her coloured tapes

Judy Right. Blue is the Condemned Cell. High window there. Door there. Another door there.
Mona (*referring to the second door*) Where does that door lead to?
Janet The gallows.
Mona Thank you.
Judy Red is the corridor. It overlaps, I'm afraid. (*She moves* R) Yellow is

the Governor's Office. Window there, overlooking the prison yard. Door there.
Harry One of those, is it?
Guy One of what?
Harry One of those depressing pieces.
Guy If you call a play about the ultimate triumph of the human spirit depressing, yes.
Harry I do. (*He picks up his toolbag*)

Guy glares at him

All right, all right. I'm just saying what I think. It won't get watched in our house, I'll tell you that.

He exits into the toilets

Guy So, to work, work, work!

Everybody retires near the coffee table, except for Mona, who wanders about in the Governor's Office

Mona!
Mona I just want to get the feel of it.
Guy But you're in the Governor's Office.
Mona I *know* I'm in the Governor's Office. I must have *been* in the Governor's Office at some stage, surely? I have to feel as though I know the place.
Guy Yes, of course, Mona.

Mona does a moody in the Governor's Office. They all wait. This completed, she moves to the Condemned Cell and sits at the table

Judy Right. Prison Officers, please.

Janet and Ellen go into the Condemned Cell and sit on the other two chairs

Terry!

Terry goes and sits in the Governor's Office. For some reason, he now wears a vicar's dog collar and bib

A Small Affair

Guy Why are you wearing that, Terry?
Terry Oh, it's my own. I thought I'd just get used to the feel of it.
Guy Will somebody tell him?
Ellen Terry, you're the Prison Governor, not the Prison Chaplain.
Terry Are you sure?

Judy thrusts a script under his nose

   I could have sworn I was the Chaplain.
Guy Well, you're not!
Terry Sorry. (*He takes the dog collar off*)
Guy Thank you. (*He reads*) "Scene One. Interior. The Governor's Office. The Governor is seated at his desk. The telephone rings."
Judy Ring-ring! Ring-ring!
Terry Where will it be?
Guy On the desk!
Terry Where on the desk?
Guy Wherever you want it! Now, will you please answer it?

Terry picks up an imaginary telephone

Terry Chaplain... Sorry. "Governor speaking... I see... No reprieve." (*He replaces the telephone, then puts his hands together*)
Guy What are you doing now, Terry?
Terry Sorry. I was going to do that as the Chaplain.
Judy Cut to Condemned Cell!
Mona "They won't hang me, will they, Mrs Brownlow? Say they won't hang me!"
Ellen (*leaning forward slightly*) "Would you like a game of draughts, dear?"
Mona Sorry, Ellen, but you're leaning in. I don't think Guy can see me. Where will my camera be, Guy?
Guy Wherever you want it to be, Mona. I shan't miss a moment.
Mona Bless you. I'm sorry, Ellen, but I do think the first close-up is so important, don't you?
Ellen I don't get any.
Mona Oh, Ellen! (*She puts a hand on Ellen's*) Guy, Ellen must have a close-up. Perhaps when I'm asleep.
Guy Good idea, Mona. Judy?

Judy makes a mark in her book

Judy Yes, Mona.
Guy And!
Mona You don't think I'm asleep too long, do you? I know Janet and Ellen's little two-hander is going to be wonderful, but are we in danger of losing the dramatic thrust?
Janet Mona, you're only asleep for six lines.
Guy Thank you, Janet. Let's talk about that scene when we come to it, shall we, Mona?
Mona Whatever you say, Guy. I'm only concerned with the piece, you know that.
Guy Of course. (*He waves a hand at Judy*) From...?
Judy (*reading*) "Would you like a game of draughts, dear?"
Mona Could that be chess? I have a feeling this girl's a chess player.
Guy Fine. Whatever you like. Ellen?
Ellen "Would you like a game of chess, dear?"
Mona (*turning to Janet*) "The reprieve will come through, won't it, Miss Parker?"
Judy Janet?
Janet I am sorry. I thought I was called Miss Harker.
Mona Parker—Harker. Does it really matter?
Janet Provided I'm called the same thing all the way through, I suppose it doesn't.
Guy What shall we settle for, Mona?

Mona gives this more consideration than it deserves

Mona I'm happier with Parker—if that's all right with Janet.

Janet alters her script

Janet Parker.
Terry I don't think she would play chess. She's only a tart after all.
Ellen Terry has a point.
Mona Bless you for the suggestion, Terry, but I want to play her as a tart with depth. Little touches like being able to play chess—a love of the ballet, perhaps. They can flesh her out.
Terry It was just a thought.

A Small Affair

Guy Thank you, Terry. And! (*He waves his hand at Judy*)
Judy (*reading*) "The reprieve will come through, won't it, Miss Parker?"
Janet "Never give up hop." Sorry—typing error. That should be "hope."
Mona May I have the line again, please?
Janet "Never give up hope."
Mona "Hope!" (*She gets up*) I feel I want to stand here, Guy. Is that all right?
Guy Whatever makes you comfortable, Mona.
Mona (*standing*) "Hope! Yes, that's what I must cling on to. Hope that I shall feel the sun on my face again!"

All the lights go out. A chorus of dismay from the actors

Guy Judy, what's happened?
Judy All the lights have gone out.
Guy (*testily*) May we find out why?

Harry comes out of the toilets

Harry Sorry, it's me, isn't it? Sit tight. I'll have you back on in a minute.

Harry goes into the toilets. We hear sobbing

Guy Is someone sobbing?
Ellen I'm sorry. It's me.
Janet Ellen, what's the matter?
Ellen It's the lights going out. Bill switches the lights off.
Janet Well, most husbands do.
Ellen He does it when I want to read in bed!
Janet Oh, dear.
Mona Men are pigs. You excluded, Guy, of course.

Terry grunts

And dear Terry.
Janet How many marriages is it now, Mona?
Mona Four. Four and three quarters. I was talking to Meryl Streep about men once, and do you know what she said? She said...

The Lights come on

Guy Excellent! Shall we press on?
Mona I hadn't finished telling you what Meryl said about men, Guy!
Guy Sorry, Mona. What did she say?
Mona She said, "Mona, men are men and women are women."

Nobody knows what to make of such a profound statement. Mona does not like the non-reaction

Well, are we getting on, or what?
Guy Yes, of course. To where we were, please.

Terry gets up and goes to the Office

Not from the beginning, Terry!
Terry Sorry. (*He goes to his chair*)
Judy "Hope. Yes, that's what I must cling on to. Hope that I shall feel the sun on my face again."
Mona (*sitting down*) "Hope! Yes, that's what I must cling on to. Hope that I shall feel the sun on my face again!"
Judy I thought you wanted to stand?
Mona Did I?
Judy Yes.
Mona Mmm. What do you think, Guy?
Guy Whatever you're comfortable with, Mona.
Mona Ellen?
Ellen I'd sit. I think I'd sit.
Mona Janet?
Janet Well, if it were me, I'd rise on the line and on "Hope that I shall feel the sun on my face again" I'd stand facing the window with my arms stretched towards the sunlight.
Mona I like that. That's inspired. Could you give me the line, Janet?
Janet "Never give up hope."
Mona "Hope!" (*She rises*) "Yes, that's what I must cling on to." (*She stands facing the window, arms outstretched*) "Hope that I shall feel the sun on my face again!"
Ellen "What about that game of——"

Mona suddenly turns

Mona You're only seeing my back, aren't you, Guy?

A Small Affair

Guy It's daring.
Mona Yes. I think I'll just stand up at the table, though. (*She moves to the table*) It was a lovely idea, Janet, but it didn't quite work, did it?
Janet No, not quite.
Guy From Ellen's line, then.
Ellen "What about that game of draughts?"
Judy "Chess."
Ellen Sorry. "What about that game of chess?"
Mona "I loved him so much. He was a swine, but I loved him!"

Ellen bursts into tears

Janet Ellen?
Mona Is she supposed to cry?
Judy Not according to the script.
Ellen I'm sorry. It was the line. It made me think of Bill.
Janet Can we stop for a minute, Guy?
Guy Yes, why not? We're doing terribly well, aren't we? Why not stop for a minute?

Terry stands up

Terry I'll just pop out, then. I need some matches.
Ellen No, really, I'm fine. I'm being silly. Let's go on, please.

Terry sighs and sits down

Mona I'll give it less. It will help Ellen. (*She gives it more*) "I loved him so much. He was a swine, but I loved him!"
Janet (*singing*) "Because he's just my Bill."

They look at Janet

  Sorry. I couldn't resist it.
Guy I wish you'd tried.
Janet Sorry. Could you give me the line again, Mona?
Mona I'd love to. "I loved him so much. He was a..."

Harry enters from the toilets

Harry Oh, you are back on again. That's good. (*He remains in the room*)
Mona (*persisting*) "I loved him so much. He was a swine, but I loved him!"
Janet "Look, Simpson——"
Harry Why do women do that?
Janet Do what?
Harry In plays. Why do women always fall for blokes who are swines?
Mona I don't need this, Guy!
Harry It's true, though, isn't it? In a play, if a woman falls for a nice bloke, you know he's going to die of something.
Guy We are not interested in your profound and expert opinions on what we are doing!
Harry I don't claim to be an expert, but I pay your licence fee and don't you forget it!
Mona Would you like my autograph?
Harry No, thanks. You take *Withering Heights*.
Terry *Wuthering*.
Harry What?
Terry It's *WUTHERING Heights*.
Harry All right. You take that. Merle Oberon marries David Niven, right? A thoroughly nice bloke. But whose arms does she choose to die in? Laurence Olivier's!
Janet No, no. You said it was the nice bloke who dies, not the heroine.
Harry It's the same principle. Women are attracted to bad lots, and that's a fact.

Ellen sobs and goes over to get a tissue from her bag

Guy Now look what you've done!
Harry I'm sorry, I'm sure. Just saying what I think.
Guy Judy?
Judy Well, do you think you could *think* what you think instead of saying it—and away from us? We are trying to rehearse.
Harry Very well. Just remember this. You're all only pretending. I'm dealing with real life in there!

Harry exits into the toilets

Mona (*scoffing*) Pretending!

A Small Affair

Ellen Well, we are really. We pretend and try to make people cry—people care. They know what crying or caring is. They do it all the time without any help from us.

This produces an uneasy silence

Mona Yes, but we—we artistes... We... (*She cannot finish the sentence*)
Judy From "Look, Simpson?"
Guy Perfect. Janet?
Janet "Look, Simpson..."
Terry I worked with David Niven once.
Janet Did you, Terry?
Terry Charming man. He bought me lunch.
Mona Paul—Paul Newman, bought me lunch—in Hollywood.
Ellen Is he nice?
Mona Magnetic. There were thirty of us at the table, but I sensed that he was really talking only to me.
Janet Did the other twenty-eight sense the same thing?
Mona Janet——
Guy Judy?
Judy "Look, Simpson."
Janet "Look, Simpson, there's no point in going back on all that happened, is there?"
Mona "Why not, Miss Harker?"
Janet I thought it was Miss Parker.
Mona *Sorry.* "Why not, Miss Parker? I've nothing left to look forward to."
Ellen "There's still the Home Secretary. There's still a chance."
Mona "Is chance a hope or is hope a chance?" What does that mean, Guy?
Guy Well, it means... It means... Judy?
Judy Search me.
Terry Ask the author.
Judy He's dead.
Terry Ah.
Mona Could I just do this? (*She attempts some expressions that interpret the line*)
Guy It's lovely. I'm not *quite* sure what it means, Mona.
Mona It makes a vague speech unnecessary. It's all on my face.
Janet In close-up?
Mona Yes, Janet, in close-up!

Terry I don't see how you can make a vague speech understandable with facial expressions if you don't know what the speech means in the first place.
Ellen Terry has a point.
Mona (*getting up*) Green Room, please, Guy!

Mona exits

Guy (*to the others*) Now look what you've done!

Guy hurries out after Mona

Terry I only said what I thought.
Janet Yes, but that's the equivalent of teaching the Pope how to pray.

Terry thinks of nipping out

Terry Well, I suppose that's break for lunch, is it?
Judy I'll make some more coffee.
Terry (*disappointed*) Oh.

Judy takes the kettle off to the toilets

Ellen Does Mona always walk out this often?
Janet She is a star, that's what you keep saying.
Terry Cicely Courtneidge would never have behaved like this.
Janet Terry, I know you're not exactly in the first flush of youth, but you couldn't have worked with Cicely Courtneidge.

Terry considers for a moment

Terry So I couldn't.

Judy comes in with the kettle. Harry follows her with a packed lunch

Judy What do you mean, "Hours"?
Harry What I say. I've never seen anything like it. Whoever wired this building had a perverted sense of humour.
Judy And what if somebody wants to go to the lavatory?

A Small Affair

Harry Take your chances in there or use another one.
Judy That's two floors down.
Janet I think our Director is going to have something to say about this.
Harry Look, he's just a television director. They're ten a penny. I'm skilled labour. I'm priceless. (*He sits down, opens his lunch and starts to eat*)
Judy You can't eat your lunch here.
Harry Well, I'm not eating it in there, am I? (*To the actors*) How's it going then?

Nobody can find an answer

> Oh. Like that.

Guy enters

Guy Mona's got a head. She's lying down. I blame all of you.

A mutinous murmur

> And it's no good muttering like the crew of the Bounty! An actress of her sensitivity needs an atmosphere to work in.

Janet She's got an atmosphere. She brings it in with her.
Terry Larry Olivier welcomed suggestions. He didn't take much notice of them, but he welcomed them.
Guy Yes, well, I didn't work with Larry Olivier, did I? And I'm surprised you can remember it. You're usually so drunk you could work with the Muppets and think they were the Royal Shakespeare Company!
Ellen Oh, shame, Guy! That's a shameful thing to say!
Guy I'm sorry, I'm sorry! I shouldn't have said that, but you don't know the pressure I'm under. (*He suddenly becomes aware of Harry*) What are you doing here?
Harry Having my lunch.
Guy We are rehearsing!
Harry No, you're not. You're arguing.
Guy Judy?
Judy Well, I don't think Mona would want him to eat in the Green Room.
Guy All right, eat your lunch! Have a banquet! (*He goes sulkily to the bed in the cell and sits on it*)

Harry I've only got cheese and pickle sandwiches. Anybody like one?
Terry That's very civil of you. (*He takes a sandwich. It is of the doorstep variety*)
Harry That's Edam, by the way. We eat a lot of Edam because my wife is actually Dutch.
Ellen I expect you call her My Old Dutch.
Harry No, I don't. I never do that.
Judy Kettle's boiling.
Terry (*to Harry*) Would you like a cup of coffee?
Harry Now, that's very civil of *you*.
Guy Look, could you just all help yourselves to coffee—two sugars for me please, Judy. We must get *on*!

Everyone helps themselves to coffee

Judy But Mona's got a head.
Guy I know Mona's got a head! Find something without Mona in it.
Terry We could do my first little scene again. No, perhaps not.
Harry What about Janet and Ellen's little two-hander?
Guy Good idea. How did you know about that?
Harry I heard somebody say.
Judy It's a good place.
Guy Thank you, Judy. That's what we'll do. Janet? Ellen?

Ellen sits at the table in the Condemned Cell. Janet stands by the bed, looking down at the imaginary sleeping figure of Mona

And!
Janet "She's asleep."
Ellen "Thank goodness. If only she could stay asleep. If only we didn't have to wake her to tell her it's time to die."

Janet sits down at the table

Janet "I haven't told you this. I've never done duty in a condemned cell before."
Ellen "I haven't told you. Neither have I."
Janet "And the prison authorities expect us to know how to deal with it. How do you deal with it?"

A Small Affair

Ellen "Pray that ultimately she can deal with it herself."

A few lines have actually been delivered properly and without interruption. It produces a small silence

Terry Bravo.
Guy But that was wonderful.
Janet Well, don't sound so surprised.
Guy Shall we run it again?
Ellen Yes, please.
Janet We'd like to.
Guy And!

Mona comes in. She overacts contrition

Mona You must all think badly of me.

Nobody denies it

No, don't deny it. And you're right. I've been a pain.

Nobody denies it

Yes, I have—and I'm sorry. I only came in from L.A.—that's Hollywood—on Wednesday. I want this piece to work above everything. I want to be one of you. Please let me be one of you!
Harry (sotto voce) Gordon Bennett!

Guy gestures to Ellen and Judy. Ellen gets the message. She gets up and hugs Mona. Janet reluctantly follows suit. Terry does his bit too, but gets a quick goose in as he does

Mona Guy!
Guy Mona!

They embrace effusively

Mona Judy!

Judy has a job. She doesn't have to do this

Judy Coffee?

A pause

Guy Well, isn't that terrific? Isn't that wonderful? We're all together again!
Mona I'm ready to work. Where are we?
Judy We were going to run the little two-hander again. You're asleep.
Mona Fine. Fine. I'm asleep. (*She goes submissively to the bed and lies down*)

Janet and Ellen resume their places

Guy And!
Janet "She's asleep."
Ellen "Thank goodness. If only she could stay asleep. If only we didn't have to wake her up to tell her it's time to die."

Janet sits at the table with Ellen. Mona decides to have a nightmare

Mona Aaaahhh!
Janet There's no "Aaaahhh!" in the script, Mona.
Mona Nobody liked it? I thought me having a nightmare was... Nobody liked it? Fine. It was only a thought.
Guy Let's crack on, shall we?
Janet "I haven't told you this. I've never done duty in the condemned cell before."

Mona starts to toss and turn on the bed

Ellen (*distracted*) "I haven't told you. Neither have I."
Janet "And the prison authorities expect us to know..." (*She sighs*)
Mona Judy! Prompt!
Janet I know the lines. I can't say the lines with you thrashing about as though you're having a multiple orgasm!
Mona Darling, I'm going to hang in the morning. I couldn't possibly sleep soundly, could I?
Harry You could have slipped some knock-out drops in her tea.
Janet That's the best idea anyone's had all morning.

A Small Affair

Terry Is it legal, though? Would wardresses be allowed to do that?
Guy Judy?
Judy What?
Guy Would they?
Judy How do I know?
Harry Look it up.
Mona Why are we listening to this man? Why is he here?
Terry He's having his lunch.
Ellen He couldn't use the Green Room because you were having a head.
Mona Oh, it's my fault, is it?
Guy Mona, if you could just sleep quietly, there's no problem.
Mona So you just want me to lie still?
Janet In close-up, of course.
Mona That's it! I've had it with her!
Janet I've got a name.
Mona Yes. Has-Been!
Janet Maybe I am, but it took me longer to become a has-been than you!

A physical confrontation looks possible. Guy gets between them

Guy Lunch! Let's break for lunch! It's a good time, isn't it?

A pause

   The others exit in sullen silence. Judy is the last to go

Guy It's all going terribly well, isn't it?
Judy *Terribly* well.

Black-out

   As the Lights come up, Ada comes into the empty room. She is a cleaner and carries a plastic sack. She starts to put the paper coffee cups into it. She starts to sing Strangers in the Night

   Harry enters from the toilets and joins in the singing

Ada Ooh!
Harry Hallo, Ada. I thought you was off at twelve?

Ada *Supposed* to be off at twelve. Not any more, though. We've been slashed.
Harry Not more cut-backs?
Ada Queenie's gone. Lily's gone.
Harry Not Lily?
Ada Nine years she'd worked here. Now they've thrown her on the slag-heap of life. How she and her husband are going to finish building their villa on the Algarve I don't know.
Harry Cut-back mad, that's what they are. You've heard they've cancelled the new serial?
Ada No?
Harry Six episodes, that's all it ran.
Ada It was just getting interesting. We'll never know who died in the fire now.
Harry Well, all of them, in a way.
Ada Mm. What's this like?

Harry puts his thumbs down

Ada Perhaps they'll cut *them* back. (*She picks up a script and looks at it*)
Harry I'd settle for them being calmed down. I can't hear myself think in there.
Ada Who writes this rubbish, anyway?

Harry picks up another script and looks at it

Harry Everard Defries, whoever he may be.
Ada Look at this for dialogue on page forty-four. Simpson: "Oh Governor. Oh Governor."
Harry (*reading from his script*) Governor: "Oh Simpson! Oh Simpson! Oh Simpson!"

They are beginning to enjoy themselves now

Harriet comes in. She is young and enthusiastic

Ada "Governor, Governor, Governor!"
Harry "Simpson, Simpson, Simpson!"

They become aware of Harriet

A Small Affair

Harriet Oh, thank goodness! Signs of life at last. I've so little time, you see. You know what editors are like. Anyway, now I've found you, may I do a piece on you?
Ada Piece?
Harriet Sorry. I haven't introduced myself. I'm Harriet Martin from *Radio Times*.
Ada Ooh!
Harriet We're doing a feature called *A Day At Rehearsal*. Well, that's the working title. I've only got a paragraph, but do you think we could do a quick interview?
Ada With us?
Harriet I'd be ever so grateful.
Harry Would we get mentioned?
Harriet Well, as the paragraph will be about you, I'd have thought that was self-evident.
Harry Yes, I suppose it would be, really.
Harriet Shall we sit?

They sit in a little group. Harriet produces a pad and a pen

I've got nothing prepared. I'll just fire off questions. Is that OK? I'll start with you...?
Ada Ada.
Harriet Ada. (*Suddenly*) *Why?*
Ada I was christened Ada.
Harriet No, no. Why do you do what you do?
Ada Well, it's a living, isn't it?
Harriet How refreshingly down to earth. Now...?
Harry Harry.
Harriet Harry. Where do you think television drama is going?
Harry Down the pan.
Harriet My God, I've struck gold here. This is wonderful stuff. Ada, do you model yourself on anybody?
Ada Not really, no. I suppose if I did, it would be Rasputin.
Harriet The Russian monk?
Ada No. My Yorkshire terrier.
Harriet I don't quite see why you'd model yourself on a Yorkshire terrier.
Ada Because he's got a lovely nature and never has a bad word to say about anybody.

Harriet That's rather sweet. Harry, here's one from left field. What's it like making love to someone you've just met?
Harry Here, that's a bit strong, isn't it?
Harriet In the job, I mean.
Harry Well, I've never come across it. You hear stories, but it's never happened to me.
Harriet Could I add, "Worse luck"?
Harry Yes, you could.
Harriet Ada, you're obviously a character lady.
Ada I have my moments.
Harry Like at the Christmas party.
Ada That was port and lemon.
Harriet No, what I mean is do you mind playing second fiddle to the stars?
Ada There's no stars in what I do.
Harriet Oh. Harry?
Harry Well, I suppose old Barry Bridges thinks he's a star, but that's only because he worked at the National last year.
Harriet What did he do—one of the classics?
Harry No. He re-wired a couple of dressing rooms.
Harriet What as?
Harry What do you mean, "What as?" As an electrician, like me.

Harriet looks appalled

Ada Did you think Harry was an actor?
Harriet Well...
Ada Him, an actor? Next thing you'll be saying is you thought I was an actress!

Harriet tries to laugh sportingly but cannot carry it off. She stands

Harriet I think I'd better go. I've made a complete fool of myself.
Harry Don't worry about it, love. People here have been doing that all morning.
Harriet I wish I'd never left the Surrey *Comet*!

Near to tears, Harriet exits

Ada and Harry take their rejection philosophically

A Small Affair

Ada So much for fame.

Harry I did wonder why she wanted to interview normal people.

Ada Talking of which, the *abnormal* lot should be back soon. I'd better be off.

Harry And I'd better get back in there. By the way, Ada, what made you call your dog Rasputin?

Ada I didn't know he was a monk. I thought he was a ballet dancer.

Harry I thought he was a goalkeeper.

He exits into the toilets

Ada prepares to leave

Caroline, a young PA, enters. She notices signs of occupation and is immediately unsure

Caroline Hi. Am I in the right room?
Ada I don't know, do I?
Caroline No, I must be in the wrong room.

Caroline exits but re-enters immediately

No, this *is* the right room. It says four-zero-three on the door and I've got four-zero-three on my sheet.
Ada Well, I'm thrilled for you.

Ada takes her plastic sack and exits

Caroline shouts out of the door

Caroline It *is* right! Would you like to come in?

Mrs Webb, Mrs Hodge, and Mrs Platt enter apprehensively

Just park yourselves anywhere. Stevie will be along in a trice.
Ladies Thank you.

They sit close together R

Caroline You've all had coffee and things?

Ladies Yes, thank you very much.
Mrs Hodge In the lounge.
Caroline That's the Green Room, actually.
Mrs Platt It wasn't green. It was a sort of slate colour.
Caroline Yes, I know, but it's called the Green Room.
Mrs Platt Why?
Caroline I don't know, actually. I'm quite new to all this. Now, does anyone have any questions?
Mrs Webb Yes, please. May I use your facilities?
Caroline Sorry?
Mrs Hodge She means your You-Know-Whats.
Caroline Oh, the lavatory? Yes, of course, just through there.
Mrs Webb Thank you very much.

Mrs Webb crosses and exits into the toilets

Mrs Platt Will we actually meet Tommy Turner today?
Caroline No, Tommy's in the studio, but if Stevie likes what you do, you'll certainly meet him next week.

A scream from the toilets

Mrs Webb rushes on

Mrs Webb There's a man in there!

Caroline picks up the internal telephone

Caroline Security? Four-zero-three. There's a prowler in the loo! (*She hangs up*)

Harry comes in

Harry I'm not a prowler. I'm Maintenance. I'm re-wiring.
Caroline Oh, I see. I am sorry.
Mrs Hodge Well, what about Mrs Webb's needs?
Harry She can't go in there. It's a death-trap in there. Two floors down's the nearest.
Mrs Webb I'd better get started.

A Small Affair

Mrs Hodge I'll come with you.
Caroline I'll show you the way. I mustn't lose you. If Stevie arrives, Mrs Platt, just introduce yourself.
Mrs Platt I'm not shy.

Caroline goes off with Mrs Webb and Mrs Hodge

Harry exits into the toilets

Mrs Platt picks up a script and sits. She reads a few lines and pulls a face

Guy enters, psyched up for the afternoon battle

Guy Who are you?
Mrs Platt I'm Ruth Platt from Romford.
Guy Aren't you a little out of your way?

Ron, the security guard, enters. He does not look particularly fearsome, but does his best to make up for it with an aggressive manner

Ron (*to Guy*) All right, sonny, out of the building!
Guy I beg your pardon?
Ron Oh, it's threats, is it?
Guy I am Guy Green!
Ron I don't care if you're Guy Fawkes, you've been reported!

Ellen and Janet come in

Janet What have you been reported for, Guy?
Guy Will you tell this fool who I am?
Ron Oh, I'm a fool now, am I? You're heading for a right bashing, you are!
Ellen He's our Director. He's Guy Green.
Guy Don't you *know* me?
Ron No.
Janet You should. He was terribly famous.
Guy *Was*?
Ron Well, I'm not interested in directors. I'm after a prowler. Somebody phoned down.
Mrs Platt That was Caroline.

Guy And where is Caroline?
Mrs Platt Taking Mrs Hodge and Mrs Webb to the You-Know-Whats two floors down.
Ron Where's this prowler then?
Mrs Platt Well, Mrs Webb thought he was in *those* You-Know-Whats, but...
Ron Right!

Ron exits into the toilets

(*Off*) All right, sonny, the game's up!
Harry (*off*) Oy! What's your game?

Ron bundles Harry in from the toilets

Ron You resist, mate, and I'll break your arm!
Ellen He's an electrician.
Ron Well, where's this prowler, then?
Mrs Platt I was trying to say. There wasn't one. It was a mistake. Mrs Webb will verify that.
Guy You see? Mrs Webb will verify that. Who's Mrs Webb?
Mrs Platt She's with me and Mrs Hodge.
Janet That explains everything.
Ron Well, I am not officially satisfied. I shall remain here until I talk to the person who called Security.
Harry Am I allowed to go back to work in the meantime?
Ron *Pro tempo*, yes.
Harry Thank you!

Harry exits into the toilets

Judy enters

Judy I can't find Terry anywhere.
Guy You tried the pub?
Judy How many pubs are there in London?
Guy Well, that's a wonderful start, isn't it?

Mona enters

A Small Affair

Mona What's a wonderful start, Guy?
Guy Nothing to worry you, Mona. Everything's fine.
Mona Oh, that's good, isn't it? Where's Terry?
Guy Judy?
Judy I think he's phoning his agent.
Mona I *do* hope it's more work. Ellen?

Mona holds out her arms. Ellen dutifully allows herself to be cuddled

Janet?

Janet grits her teeth and follows suit. Mona opens her arms towards Judy. Judy busies herself looking at the script, but Ron is in Mona's eye-line and thinks she means him. He comes forward and embraces Mona rather stiffly

Bless you, but who are you?
Ron I'm Ron. I'm Security.

Mona turns to Guy

Mona Oh, Guy, that is *so* sweet of you!
Guy What?
Mona You must have guessed that I always had personal security in Hollywood, and you've laid on Ron.
Ron Laid on?
Guy Judy?

Judy beckons Ron towards her. She slips him a tenner. Ron shrugs and sits down

Mrs Platt (*to Mona*) Excuse me, but I know you.
Mona How kind. (*She dashes off her autograph and gives it to Mrs Platt*)
Mrs Platt Thank you.
Mona (sotto voce) Who *is* she?
Ellen Mrs Platt.
Janet She's with Mrs Webb and Mrs Hodge.
Mona Guy?
Guy Judy?

Judy Right. I don't wish to be rude, Mrs Platt, but who exactly are you?
Mrs Platt I might be a contestant on *Make a Fool of Yourself*.
Judy That's a game show.
Mrs Platt I know.
Ellen I think you're in the wrong room, dear.
Janet Oh, I don't know.
Mrs Platt I was told to wait.
Ron (*to Mona*) Would you like me to frogmarch her out, madam?
Mrs Platt You touch me and you'll get my handbag round your head!
Mona Ron, it's all right. Mrs Platt is a fan and I've always been accessible.

Janet chokes on a laugh. Ron returns to his seat, still making vague threatening gestures

The door opens and Caroline comes in. Seeing all the people, she looks apologetic

Caroline Sorry. Wrong room.

She goes out

Guy Who was that?
Judy I don't know.

Caroline enters

Caroline It *is* the right room! It's four-zero-three and there's Mrs Platt. It *is* the right room. Why am I always so willing to believe I'm wrong?
Judy Because in this case, you are!
Caroline But Stevie booked the room.
Judy Then *Stevie's* wrong.
Caroline No. Stevie's never wrong. Come in Mrs Hodge—Mrs Webb. Sit down.

Mrs Hodge and Mrs Webb enter and sit beside Mrs Platt

Guy Judy! Get me the Head of Drama!
Caroline We're Light Entertainment!
Guy Judy?

Caroline There's Stevie now.

Stevie comes in. She is a very together lady

Stevie (*to Guy*) What are you doing in my rehearsal room?
Guy This is *my* rehearsal room.
Stevie Prove it!
Guy I have a cast. We've been here since this morning.
Stevie Well, I have it from two o'clock onwards.
Guy You most certainly do not!
Ellen I think there's been a mix-up.
Janet I think there are more of *us*.
Guy (*to Stevie*) Now, my dear girl, listen to reason.
Stevie Don't you "dear girl" me, you old handbag!
Mrs Webb If we just went...

The three ladies stand

Stevie Stay where you are!

They sit. Stevie and Caroline line up on their side. Guy and Judy do the same with their actors. It looks like a stand-off

Harry comes out of the toilets with his bag

Harry All done. Afternoon, all!

This is greeted by total silence

Manners? Whatever happened to them?

He goes out

Stevie resolves to take over

Stevie (*to her ladies*) Right! Now, would you all like to tell me what you're going to do in *Make A Fool Of Yourself*?
Mrs Platt Well, I juggle with eggs, but I'm not that good and they're raw, so they go all over the place.

The actors' side is stunned

Caroline Could you sort of get some on you?
Mrs Platt Oh yes. Easily.
Stevie Mrs Hodge?
Mrs Hodge I sing *One Night Of Love* and eat an entire jelly while I'm doing it.
Caroline Do you spill quite a lot down your front?
Mrs Hodge All the time.
Stevie I like it. Mrs Webb?
Mrs Webb I play the xylophone on stilts.
Caroline You fall off a lot, presumably?
Mrs Webb No. I'm very good on stilts, believe it or not.
Stevie With respect, Mrs Webb, that's hardly making a fool of yourself.
Mrs Webb Oh, it is, because I'm not very good on the xylophone.

Even Stevie has to think about this one. Mona suddenly gets up and goes to her chair in the cell

Mona "Why not, Miss Parker? I've nothing left to look forward to!"

Rallying to the colours, Ellen and Janet rush to their places

Ellen "There's still the Home Secretary. There's still a chance."
Mona "Is hope a chance or is chance a hope?"
Janet "Listen, listen! It's the Governor!"

Terry, very much the worse for wear, staggers in and crosses up to Stevie

Terry "I'm sorry, Simpson. There's no reprieve!" (*He tries to clutch Stevie for support, but collapses*)

Black-out

As the Lights come up, the two sides face each other in hostile silence. Terry is now laid out on the bed

Sally enters. She is a young earnest woman from administration

A Small Affair

Sally Mr Plant's apologies, but he can't come down himself. His knee's gone again. I'm his assistant, Sally Purvis, actually designated as Administrative Assistant to the Head of Administration.

Guy I am Guy Green—director.

Stevie And I am Stevie Weston—*Executive* Producer.

Sally Good. Well, the thing is this. There has been a mistake.

Janet Do tell.

Caroline It's me, isn't it? I *did* get the wrong room, didn't I?

Sally Well, no actually. It was Administration. It was an administrative error by an administrative secretary.

Stevie You?

Sally No. I am an Administrative Assistant. The error, as I have previously said was by an Administrative Secretary, which is a different administrative grade. Administration, you see, is a highly structured department and——

Judy *Who gets the room?*

Sally Ah. Well, you do—for today.

Guy What do you mean, "for today"?

Caroline And what am I supposed to do? See prospective contestants in the car park?

Sally Oh no. This was the administrative error to which I referred earlier. You are actually supposed to be in room three-zero-four.

Caroline That's four-zero-three backwards!

Sally So it is.

Stevie Very well. I shall, of course, be writing a formal letter of complaint to you about the inconvenience you have caused.

Sally I understand your point of view, of course, but there's really no point. As I pointed out, I am an Administrative Assistant and any complaint should actually be directed to the Head of Administration. If it came to me as Administrative Assistant, I could only——

Stevie All right, all right! We shall move to room three-zero-four.

Guy As quickly as possible, please!

Stevie It's a bigger room, anyway.

Stevie exits

Caroline Fine. Mrs Webb, Mrs Hodge, Mrs Platt—if you'd like to follow me.

The ladies get up

Room three-zero-four, room three-zero-four.

She exits

Mrs Webb Very nice to have met you all.
Mrs Hodge Good luck with your thing.

Mrs Webb and Mrs Hodge exit

Guy *Thing?*

Mrs Platt gives Mona her autograph

Mrs Platt I think you'd better have your autograph back.
Mona My dear woman, this silly little scene is none of your doing.
Mrs Platt No, I know, only, you aren't who I thought you were, anyway.

Mrs Platt exits

Mona crumples the paper

Mona I'm beginning to wish I'd never agreed to do this play.
Guy Oh, don't say that, Mona.
Janet I agree with her.
Mona Now, look, Janet... You agree with me?
Janet Yes. It's got a curse on it.
Ellen Oh, don't say that!
Guy Yes, come on, troops. Where's our *esprit de corps*?

Judy points at Terry

Judy I think he sums it up quite perfectly.
Guy Well, see if you can wake him up!
Judy (*shaking Terry*) Terry!

Magically galvanized, Terry jumps to his feet

Terry "Now is the winter of our discontent made glorious summer by this son of York!"

A Small Affair

Mona Doctor Theatre!
Janet Not quite. He's doing *Richard The Third*.
Terry Are we breaking for lunch?
Guy We've had lunch and yours was obviously liquid! Now pull yourself together, Terry.
Judy I'll make some coffee.

Judy exits into the toilet to fill the kettle

The phone rings

Guy Judy?
Judy (*off*) I'm filling the kettle!

Guy answers the phone

Guy Guy Green. (*He is immediately alarmed*) What? When? I see. Why? No, of course he will. (*He hangs up*)

Judy enters with the kettle

The Head of Drama's coming over!
Judy Why?
Guy His secretary didn't know.
Mona Well, I think it's wonderful. He obviously realises that this is a prestigious production and wants to declare his personal interest.
Guy Yes, yes, that's it! Of course!
Janet If he's going to declare his personal interest, hadn't we better show him something to be interested *in*?
Ellen We should be rehearsing!
Janet Yes, Ellen.
Mona I remember Steve—Steve Spielberg coming down to the set. He was incredibly supportive.
Terry I shall be fine as soon as I've had some coffee, I know I shall.
Guy Right! Then it's onwards and upwards. Where were we, Judy?
Judy That's open to debate.
Ellen Hadn't Terry just come in to say there was no reprieve?
Judy Yes, but he said it to Stevie.
Janet And then passed out.

The phone rings and Judy answers it

Judy Four-zero-three. Ron? Oh, Ron.

Everyone realises that Ron is still with them

It's for you.

Ron goes to pick up the telephone

Ron Ron here. Oh, hallo, Ron. Right. OK, Ron. (*He hangs up*) Ron wants me at the front desk.
Terry I thought you were Ron.
Ron Yes, I am, but Ron's a Ron as well. The thing is, the Head of Drama's coming over, so we need to be at full strength at the front desk.
Guy Then go.
Ron Yes, but I thought...
Mona Bless you *for* the thought, Ron, but you pop along. Perhaps you'd see me into my car this evening, if people have gathered.
Ron What people?
Mona Fans.
Ron Fans?
Guy Goodbye, Ron.
Ron I'm glad you kept the room. I don't like that *Make a Fool of Yourself*. It's just people making fools of themselves, isn't it?

Ron exits, to a beaming smile from Mona

Guy Right, then. We're off and running again. Places as before, please.

Mona, Ellen and Janet sit in the Condemned Cell. Terry hovers nearby

Terry Am I in or out at this stage?
Guy Judy?
Judy It depends where we're going from.
Mona I thought perhaps my speech?
Guy Good idea. Corridor, please, Terry. And!
Mona "Why not, Miss Harker?"
Janet Parker.

A Small Affair

Mona "Parker. I've nothing left to look forward to."
Ellen "There's still the Home Secretary. There's still a chance."
Mona "Is hope a chance or hope a chance?"
Janet "Listen! Listen! It's the Governor!"

Judy cues Terry in, and he makes his entrance

Terry "I'm sorry, Simpson. There's no——"
Janet How do I know it's the Governor? I say "Listen, listen, it's the Governor", but all I'm hearing is the footsteps.
Ellen It is a point.
Mona Yes, it's false. I can't stand anything that's false.
Janet We know, Mona, we know.
Guy Mm. It's a tricky one, this. How does Janet know it's the *Governor's* footsteps?

They all think deeply

Terry I could have a limp.
Guy Pardon?
Terry A limp. If I had a limp, the sound of my footsteps would be quite distinctive. (*He demonstrates*) Instead of... (*He takes regular footsteps*) I'd have... (*He takes irregular footsteps*)
Guy Sounds good to me. Janet?
Janet Fine.
Terry I'll come back in then, shall I?
Guy If you would, please, Terry.

Terry goes to the corridor

Terry From?
Guy Judy?
Judy "Listen! Listen! It's the Governor!"
Janet "Listen! Listen! It's the Governor!"

Terry starts to limp down the corridor

Ellen Shouldn't Terry be on the move before Janet says the line?
Janet Yes. Otherwise I'm saying "Listen, listen", and I still haven't heard anything.

Mona My own thoughts exactly.
Guy Back you go, Terry.

Terry goes back to his position

Judy?
Judy Cue Terry's limp!

Terry limps heavily down the corridor

Cue Janet!
Janet "Listen! Listen! It's the Governor!"

Terry comes into the cell

Terry "I'm sorry, Simpson..."
Mona "How's your leg today, Governor?"
Terry Pardon?
Guy Why are you saying that, Mona?
Mona It just came to me. I think it's a wonderful opportunity to show what a caring character Simpson is. Even when her life is hanging by a thread, she's concerned about the Governor's leg.
Janet She *is* a murderess.
Mona A crime of passion, Janet. I still think she'd care about people with limps. Guy?
Guy Fine, Mona, but we must crack on.
Terry Shall I limp down the corridor again?
Guy No! Be *in*! And!
Terry "I'm sorry, Simpson."
Mona "How's your leg today, Governor?"
Terry "There's no reprieve." That sounds rather harsh doesn't it? Simpson enquires about his leg and he just says, "No reprieve."
Janet It's ambiguous as well. Terry saying "No reprieve" could mean no reprieve from the pain in his leg.
Terry Am I in constant pain? Judy?
Judy How should I know? You didn't even have a bad leg five minutes ago!
Terry Because if I *am* in constant pain, it would show on my face. The pain would be etched.
Mona Wouldn't that be distracting—for all of us?

A Small Affair

Ellen I know! What if Terry said, "Good-morning" first? Then Mona could ask him about his leg and then he could say "Very well, thank you", or something—I'm not a writer—and *then* he could say "I'm sorry, Simpson, there's no reprieve."
Guy Does that work for you, Terry?
Terry Yes, that's fine.
Guy Mona? Mona?
Mona Sorry, Guy. I was just thinking.

Everybody looks worried

Guy What were you thinking, Mona?
Mona Well, I still want to be caring, but wouldn't it be wonderfully ironic if, instead of a bad leg, Terry had a bad neck?
Guy Why?
Mona Don't you see? I am a woman facing the gallows and wonderfully ironically I say, "Good-morning, Governor. How's your neck?"

A stunned silence

You all hate it?
Guy Well...
Janet He's got to have a limp, Mona. I've got to recognise the footsteps.
Ellen Perhaps he could whistle. If he always whistled the same tune, Janet could recognise the whistle.
Janet Whistling on his way to a condemned cell?
Ellen Perhaps not.
Guy Are you really keen on the bad neck line, Mona?
Mona I'm only thinking of the piece.
Guy Of course you are. Terry?
Terry I limp and have a stiff neck?
Judy He'll look like Quasimodo.
Guy Let's try it, shall we? From the corridor, please, Terry.

Terry takes his place. Then he comes down the corridor. He limps, adopts a stiff neck and whistles

We're not doing the whistling, Terry.
Terry Sorry. I'll go back. (*He goes back to the corridor*)

Head of Drama comes in

Judy (sotto voce) Head of Drama!

Guy immediately looks terrified

Head Of Drama No, no—carry on, please. I shan't interrupt.
Guy Thank you very much. Judy?
Judy Cue Terry!

Terry, with a limp and a stiff neck, comes along the corridor. Head of Drama's eyes widen

Judy Cue cell!
Mona "Why——"
Head Of Drama Why is the Prison Governor deformed?
Guy It does emerge in the text.
Head Of Drama I see. Go on, please.
Judy Mona?
Mona "Why not Miss Harker?"
Janet "Parker."
Mona "Parker! I've nothing left to look forward to."
Ellen "There's still a chance. There's still the Foreign Secretary."
Head Of Drama *Foreign* Secretary?
Ellen "Home"—sorry. "There's still a Home Secretary." No! "There's still a chance."
Mona (*giving it the gun*) "Is hope a chance or is chance a hope?"

Terry moves too soon and will be standing outside the door by the time Janet has spoken

Janet "Listen! Listen! It's the Governor!"
Terry (*realising his error*) Ah.
Guy (*to Head of Drama*) He moved early. We will hear the limp!

Head of Drama nods

Well, in you go, Terry!

Terry goes into the Condemned Cell

A Small Affair

Terry "There's no reprieve!"
Mona "Good-morning, Governor. How's your neck?"
Terry Oh. "It's very well, thank you. Good-morning."
Mona "Good-morning, Governor. How's your leg?"
Terry "It's very well, thank you. I'm sorry, Simpson, there's no reprieve. My neck's very well, too."
Mona "No reprieve! I'm going to die!"(*She flings herself on the bed. The dramatic effect is marred when she bounces straight off the other side and disappears*)
Janet We just did, dear.

Guy turns to Head of Drama

Guy And that's as far as we've got. But we have had a very torrid day of it. We've had electricians and security men——
Ellen Ron.
Guy Yes, Ron. Then there was a mix-up over the room and we had Admin down—stray contestants for *Make a Fool of Yourself*.
Head Of Drama Really? One of my favourite programmes.
Guy Oh, mine too. But they were all contributory factors, you see. I mean, under normal circumstances we'd be in much better shape than this. Still, we've got two weeks' rehearsal, and I'm sure we'll go from strength to strength.
Head Of Drama Ah. Well, actually it's the two weeks' rehearsal I wanted to talk to you about.
Guy You're not cutting it?
Head Of Drama Not so much cutting it as cancelling it. I'm sorry. The whole thing is cancelled.

Everyone is aghast

Guy Cancelled?

Mona surfaces from behind the bed

Mona *Us?*
Head Of Drama It's the cut-backs, you see. I'm having to cut back on our Drama output.
Janet But why us?

Head Of Drama Well, let's be honest, it isn't the greatest script in the world. My Deputy popped it into the slot when I was in Montreux. Quite frankly, I would never have let it out of the starting gate myself.

Mona limps back to join them

Mona But I can be wonderful in it. We can all be wonderful in it.
Head of Drama Oh, I'm sure you would have been. From what I saw, you were already rising above the material. But, as I said, something had to go and it's you. I *am* sorry.

Head of Drama exits, leaving them stunned

Terry It was a rotten play, anyway.
Ellen Yes, a really rotten play.
Judy It would never have stood up.
Guy I didn't say so, but I always had doubts. I could strangle the author!
Judy You'd have to dig him up first.
Mona Well, I believed in it! It could have... All right, I *wanted* to believe in it.
Janet We all *wanted* to believe in it. If you're out of work, you want to believe in anything you're offered.
Mona Oh, I don't need the work. It's just that good leading roles are a little scarce these days. I only made one film in Hollywood, you know. They call them Bummers over there.

Janet touches Mona's hand

Ellen I was just looking forward to two weeks away from home.
Guy I shall, of course, resign!
All No, you won't.
Guy No, I won't.

They laugh. In defeat there is a camaraderie which was never there before

Well, it's been horrific. Let's all do something else together sometime.
Janet We might get *two* days rehearsal next time.
Ellen So now we all go home, I suppose?
Mona No, we do not! We all go to my house, drink champagne, and damn the Drama Department to eternity, or until they employ us again.

Judy I'd better clear up.
Guy We'll come back tomorrow, Judy—disrupt somebody else's rehearsal.

Thrown together by misfortune, they exit as friends

Terry is the last to move, but he stops and looks around, aware that this may be the last rehearsal he will ever attend

Mona comes back for him

Mona Terry?
Terry You know, I don't get many apt lines these days, but I had one today.
Mona What was that?
Terry No reprieve.
Mona Shall we limp?

They smile at each other and exit, limping

CURTAIN

FURNITURE AND PROPERTY LIST

Further dressing may be added at the director's discretion

On stage: Chairs
Small table. *On it:* electric kettle, jar of coffee, bag of sugar, tin of biscuits, plastic spoons, lots of paper cups
Small wheeled table. *On it:* stop-watch, little tub of different coloured pens, scripts, coloured tape
Internal telephone
Bed

Off stage: Executive briefcase (**Guy**)
Bag. *In it:* bottle of brandy, dog-collar (**Terry**)
Toolbag (**Harry**)
Bag. *In it:* tissues (**Ellen**)
Packed lunch (cheese and pickle sandwiches) (**Harry**)
Plastic sack (**Ada**)

Personal: **Terry:** dark glasses
Harriet: pad, pen
Judy: ten pound banknote
Mona: pen, paper

LIGHTING PLOT

Property fittings required: nil
Interior. The same scene throughout

To open: Overall general lighting

Cue 1	**Mona**: "…feel the sun on my face again!" *Fade lights out*	(Page 13)
Cue 2	**Mona**: "She said…" *Bring up lights*	(Page 13)
Cue 3	**Judy**: *"Terribly* well." *Black-out, then bring up lights when ready*	(Page 23)
Cue 4	**Terry** collapses *Black-out, then bring up lights when ready*	(Page 34)

EFFECTS PLOT

Cue 1   **Guy** almost picks up the phone   (Page 2)
          Phone rings

Cue 2   **Judy** exits into the toilet   (Page 37)
          Phone rings

Cue 3   **Janet**: "And then passed out."   (Page 37)
          Phone rings

PRINTED IN GREAT BRITAIN BY
THE LONGDUNN PRESS LTD., BRISTOL.